Connecting Horizons with Job

Pastoral Care (in Cooperation with Professionals) in the Trauma-Coping Process

By
Egbert Brink

WILLIAM CAREY INTERNATIONAL UNIVERSITY PRESS

WCJU

press

William Carey International University Press

1539 E. Howard Street, Pasadena, California 91104

E-mail: wciupress@wciu.edu

www.wciupress.org

Author: Egbert Brink
Connecting Horizons with Job

ISBN: 9780865850767

Library of Congress Control Number: 2013944339

Printed in the United States of America

CONTENTS

IMAGES

Foreword

Trauma is one of the major challenges of our generation. The situation seems to become worse everyday. The effects of September 11 are still visible. Terrorism continues to hit various parts of our globe. Shooting in schools and other public venues are becoming more frequent. Many countries and regions are going through civil wars with all the tragic losses, rapes and other barbaric acts that accompany them. Famine, natural catastrophes, socio-political troubles, organized social violence, persecution, economic crises and much more push many populations into deep distress and unimaginable turmoil. The skyrocketing divorce rate and its damaging effects on families is a serious and multifaceted threat to our human societies. Even in regions where people seem to live a normal life, personal physical, moral or spiritual challenges can hit anytime and bring serious disturbance. Stress that comes with a more demanding workplace or market can also be overwhelming. For these reasons, it is very important to have a better understanding of the phenomenon and to learn how to properly cope with it. But finding the right response is a very complicated endeavor. Psychiatrists have a variety of views and so do religious leaders. Could it be that the solution lies more in an interdisciplinary approach?

Here is where Dr Egbert Brink's contribution is very important. He is one of the most gifted pastors I have ever known. He is also an author and a scholar who skillfully balances his pastoral ministry with his teaching loads in various universities within his country, the Netherlands, and overseas. Furthermore, he has the wisdom to work with professionals as he meets the felt need of people around him who are dealing with trauma.

This book balances theory and practice very well. The hermeneutical framework based on the book of Job is very inspiring. The illustrations are very helpful. Above all, the practical recommendations to pastoral counselors as they accompany counselees in their battle with stress deserve to be taken seriously as they come not only from a person who has studied the phenomenon but also an experienced pastor who learned to work with mental health professionals.

Every pastor, mental health professional and educator must read this study.

Moussa Bongoyok, PhD
Faculty member at Biola University
Major Advisor at William Carey International University
Founder of the Francophone University of International Development

Preface

In the summer of 2012 I completed my study on "Trauma counseling with the use of the Book of Job" in close collaboration with workers in the field of mental health. It was the explicit wish of the counselee (henceforth referred to by the pseudonym Naomi) to share the help she received with respect to trauma, religion and pastoral care with the wider public. Her wish is to be of benefit to others by allowing use of the material produced during the creative therapy as long as the specifics of her case history were not revealed. She also allowed me to make use of her written reflections on the pastoral sessions. These reflections were continually shared with the creative therapist Jolanda Glas for synchronization of care. It is my living hope that this case-study may contribute to a growing collaboration between pastoral (spiritual) counselors and psychological therapists, with respect to each specific domain.

I thank Dr. Moussa Bongoyok for his special recognition and his efforts to make it possible to obtain with this study a ThD after enrolling in a condensed doctorate program at Promise Christian University. This study was part of the evidence that I met the academic requirements after a proper academic evaluation of my academic training, publications and almost 25 years of teaching experience and pastoral ministry. I wish to thank the translators Sabrine Bosscha-Timmermans, Paul Waterval and my friend Rev. Donald Cowart for their contribution. I am also grateful to Heather Holt of William Carey International University — in close cooperation with Promise — who stimulated me to publish this study for the larger public.

I thank the living God for my wife and the four children that He gave me, and for so much (multicultural) friendship. Without the fullest confidence and loving support from my wife Mirjam, I would certainly not be arriving at this stage. She has a noble character and is worth far more than rubies. I especially wish to thank the Triune God for His divine direction in my life. His Name is infinitely multifaceted and unsurpassed. After all those pastoral routes with traumas I do recognize with Job: 'My ears had heard of you, but now my eyes have seen you' (Job 42:5), in the light of Christ!

Egbert Brink, ThD

4 July 2013, Waddinxveen, The Netherlands

Introduction[1]

The pastoral care provider can make a specific contribution to the trauma coping process alongside other professionals. This conviction has been increasingly advocated in recent publications (Van den Blink 2010, 20)[2] (Wright 2011). Dr. Ruard Ganzevoort, for instance, argues that the trained pastoral counselor is a specialist in his own right dealing with aspects such as personal philosophy and meaning. In addition to the important task of identifying and referring the trauma patient to the proper specialists, he is also to act from his own competence within the religious domain (Ganzevoort 2011, 2).

What, then, can a pastoral or spiritual counselor specifically contribute to the trauma healing process? I asked myself this question when I was approached by a church member for pastoral care. She was severely traumatized. This initiated my research within the field of pastoral care, in close cooperation with mental health specialists and the counselee herself.

After my counselee had been referred to a psychiatric care unit where she was diagnosed with Post-Traumatic Stress Disorder

1 Parts of this paper were published earlier in the article 'Pour une approche pastorale dans le contexte post-traumatique' in *La Revue réformée* 60, no. 251 (2009).
2 Aforementioned article is partly a reflection of 'Trauma Reactivation in Pastoral Counseling: Implications for Theory and Practice' in *American Journal of Pastoral Counseling* 1, 2, (1998): 23–39.

(DSM IV, TR, 2001), several consultations took place between a Creative Arts Therapist, Jolanda Glas, and myself as pastor. She put me on the trail of some illuminating literature from her field of expertise[3], whereby I made use of Judith Herman's main work (Herman 2001) as well as, at a later stage, the broader orientated *Trauma: diagnostiek en behandeling* (Aarts and Visser 2007), including the sections on neuroscience by Dutch specialists. The close cooperation between our varying disciplines proved to be mutually enriching and beneficial for the counselee.

Purpose

In the first section, a description of the type of trauma is given and of the phase in which the trauma coping process was taking place, while respecting the wish of the counselee not to offer an explicit case description. Thereafter the search for and development of an effective pastoral approach will be explained. Then a motivation for reading the Book of Job will follow, concluded with a description of the hermeneutic method in the pastoral setting. In the second section, a *component* of the pastoral approach followed will be described. It is an account of that spiritual counseling process which was synchronized as much as possible with creative therapy. A specific hermeneutical approach to the Book of Job (trauma and theodicy) played an important role. Reading the book Job proved to be an effective means to connect with the suffering of the counselee.

---

3 Creative therapy has proved to be of benefit to people who have been traumatized at an early age because an immediate event is better expressed in a visual manner than with words. Also, the sensorial sensations accompanying drawing and painting, like the scratching of a pencil or chalk, and experiencing the colors, make it easier to connect with the past (Wertheim-Cahen 2007, 313).

Chapter 1: Type II Trauma

T rauma is too general a specification. The literature on trauma distinguishes various types[4]. Within PTSD a distinction is now being made, based on the kind of trauma, between a 'single incident' Type I and a chronic Type 2 PTSD. The case at hand is not about coping with a single traumatic event, which can cause a stress disorder. In this case we are dealing with (what Herman calls) a complex post-traumatic stress disorder, i.e. Type 2. In this type one or more deeply traumatic events form a prolonged threat to the physical (and mental) integrity of the person involved. The case at hand concerns sudden loss through death and different kinds of abuse. The term 'complex' is also in place here because, in addition to the traumatic events, the counselee's personality and situation also play a role. It concerns a chronic form of PTSD.

Incapable of integrating her memories of overwhelming events, Naomi was passionately in search of a safe place. Past traumatic experiences could be activated suddenly and unpredictably by what was taking place in the present. The cause of these flashbacks was not always clear and difficult to ascertain. Numerous 'triggers' could reactivate the trauma. Her state shifted constantly between hypervigilance, arousal and emotional numbness (apathy). [5]

4 Ganzevoort 2005, 345 with reference to the summary in *Trauma: diagnostiek en behandeling*, 2007.
5 According to Herman, the many symptoms of PTSD can be divided into three main categories of hyper-arousal, intrusion, and constriction: hyper-activation,

In order to cope, people with PTSD bury their memories of the trauma as deeply as possible. They often have isolated their emotions from their cognitions resulting in an emotional numbness. *Trauma, it freezes thinking* (Wright 2011, 198). All situations that could possibly bring to mind the traumatic event are avoided as much as possible. Memories are accompanied by pain and so are blocked out.

The material presented in the second section stems from the first phase of the traumatic recovery process, in which dissociation (dissociating from the feelings evoked by painful experiences) was common. Gradually the transition was made into the second phase, designated by Herman as: remembrance and mourning, reconnection and communality (Herman 2001, 201–302).

Pastoral approach

In order to help traumatized people, a pastor must realize that the quality of his relationship with the counselee is of the utmost importance (Blink Van den 2010 referring to Blink Van den 2004). First and foremost, it is a matter of providing safety (holding environment)[6]. Of course the professional code of confidentiality offers protection, but that in itself is not enough. Safety must also become apparent within the relationship. For example, the pastor should *never* take the initiative to approach the traumatic events. While a concerned interest from a serving and listening attitude is beneficial, curiosity (a search for sensation), on the other hand, is harmful and will create an unsafe setting[7]. Traumatized people are especially in need of extra

continuous expectation of danger; obsessive re-experiencing, indelible imprint of the trauma; numbness, someone who is forced to surrender becomes numb (Herman 2001, 35).

6 The expression is borrowed from Winnicott (Winnicott 1960). The holding environment in a sense represents reality. If the environment is a good holding environment, it makes a person feel taken care of and protected.

7 Recent research has proved that probing questioning does not help. Forcing

protection before they themselves dare to approach the traumas. Whether they ever reach the stage where they are able to share those experiences is not a given fact.

Safety should also include a *sense of security.* Trauma literarily means: serious injury. The purpose is to provide attentive care to the wound, fully recognizing the seriousness of the injury. Unfortunately, people with traumatic experiences are often wounded further by misunderstanding and insensitive reactions to their pain and sorrow. A sense of security makes it easier to express confused feelings and allows the counselee to address God with the most penetrating why-questions.

In addition to safety and security, it is also necessary to give the counselee space so that autonomy can take shape. Because the traumatized person is frequently overwhelmed by feelings of helplessness and powerlessness, great effort is required to stimulate and challenge a sense of autonomy. After all, it is characteristic of traumatic events that the victim has little or no control over the situation whatsoever. The safe environment was violated and because of the trauma the person involved was not in control. As a result, trust in others and in one's self can be seriously damaged, and also challenge one's trust in God.[8]

After twenty years of experience as a pastor, it has become clearer to me how essential it is that the spiritual counselor provides space for transformation, never dominating or interposing oneself, but following and walking alongside. The image of a caterpillar wrestling to emerge from a cocoon as a butterfly comes to mind. Outside intervention will obstruct the ability to fly. The butterfly's struggle to leave the cocoon provides it with the life-blood and

people to talk about their traumatic experiences can not only aggravate the situation but also bring the risk of renewed trauma. (Van den Blink, 2010, 27)
8 Problematic conceptions of God often go hand in hand with problematic experience of the self. (Roukema-Koning 1998, 43–64).

strength it needs to fly (Bommerez 2008, 23–25)[9]. Therefore, as pastor, it is important to adopt an attitude of empathic *accompanying* of the counselee in his or her search, fully respecting the boundaries set by that other. The counselee must maintain full control over what he or she wishes to share.

Since anxieties of all sorts play such an important role, the attitude recommended by Edwin Friedman in the leadership field is very useful here. He speaks of a *'non-anxious presence'* that does not allow itself to be led by fear and which shuns any 'quick-fix' (Friedman 2007, 172–186) seeking to solve, remove or 'deal with' a matter. For this reason I prefer the term 'coping with trauma' to 'dealing with trauma' — as if it can be dealt with (Matsakis 1992).[10] The aim is to connect with the counselee and offer him or her the possibility to allow also a connection with his or her suffering, in order to perforate the isolation and lessen the loneliness.

In the trauma coping process it is of the utmost importance to integrate and learn to use memories. This became possible because the counselee started to learn to connect with her memories, with her pain and anxiety, and at times with unspeakable suffering. The pastor can be of assistance in making this connection, without himself taking over the suffering! (Only the great Pastor, Jesus Christ, is capable of doing that. He makes connections in a way no one else can, and shuns no suffering).

Trauma and Job

During our first pastoral conversations, I suspected that the

---

9 Also to be found on various English websites (www.forwardsteps.com.au/but-terflylesson.html by unknown author), but originally from the Netherlands.
10 Neuro-scientific research has proved that it is impossible to cope with an event to the point that the painful experience is no longer activated. It is, however, possible to develop a new manner of behavior (coping) and of association with others (Van den Blink 2010, 26) (Siegel 1999)

Book of Job contained elements that might aid Naomi to find new openings in her suffering and to connect with her wounded self, to look in this way for connections with God, others, self, and the experience of suffering. The language of Job in the jargon of the experience of death could prove helpful in approaching the trauma (Mathewson 2006).

Why Job? The Book of Job deals with the trauma of suffering.[11] Although it is hard to say if Job himself was traumatized or suffered from PTSD, the events that took place in his life were clearly traumatic: the loss of his wealth and possessions, the sudden death of his children, the disintegration of his health. His safe world has been shattered and is no longer a place of refuge — and that is not all: traumas are also caused by the reactions of those surrounding the victim. Initially his friends reacted suitably by sitting seven days at his side in silence, because they saw how great his suffering was (Job 2:13)[12]. This gives Job such a sense of security that he vents his feverish grief by cursing his day of birth (Job 3:1 'After this'!). It does not remain that way, however, because the friends maintain a logic similar to that of Mrs. Job who abandoned him. Her reasoning is as follows: the disasters that overcame them cannot be Job's fault as she knows him to be a man of great integrity, thus it must be God's fault. Therefore she bids God farewell and disappears from the story (Job 2:1–10). Job can expect no attempted connection and no security from her. The three friends (Eliphaz, Bildad and Zophar) apply the same logic but in the opposite direction: all that happened to

---

11 Mathewson states that in his speeches Job articulates his experience of suffering as the experience of death. He refers to the observations of Robert J. Lifton (Lifton 1979): 'survivors of disaster often sense that their world has "collapsed" and they engage in a struggle to go on living. Part of this struggle involves finding meaning in death and locating death's place in the continuity of life' (Mathewson 2006).

12 Unless otherwise indicated, all Scripture quotations and references are taken from the New International Version of the Bible (NIV 1984)

Job cannot be God's fault, so the cause must lie with Job himself. They act as God's defenders.

Job is attacked from all sides in his suffering. He is longing for compassion, that his anguish and misery should be weighed (Job 6:2). In the beginning the Name of God is his refuge like a fortified tower (Job 1:21, cf. Proverbs 18:10), but that becomes more and more difficult to maintain. Job experiences God as an Adversary (Job 6:4; 23:6), complains and cries out his suffering to God. He is, in fact, cornered and makes a passionate appeal to God as his advocate (=*melits*) 'against' God… (Job 16:19–21) (De Jong 1994, 37–48)! Elihu continues along the same line, talking about a mediator (*melits*), one out of a thousand (Job 33:23–24). Yet Job is told that, despite his pugnacity, he spoke justly of God, in contrast to his friends (Job 42:8). By recompensing Job with twice the amount he lost, God indirectly admits that Job had been robbed (cf. Ex 22:9)[13]. God takes the highest responsibility (Van de Beek 1992) and recognizes that all that happened to Job was without any demonstrable reason (Job 2:3): Job as the suffering righteous person.

The most pertinent question to Job is: 'would you discredit my justice? Would you condemn me to justify yourself' (Job 40:8). It is not the point that Job had not the right to justify himself, but that he defended his right at the expense of God's justice. Neither the logic of his friends and the logic of his wife sustain, and Job's logic also fails. God's justice would be in Job's vision: people get what they deserve, the righteous will prosper and the evil will be punished. Job did not get what he deserved

13 'The one whom the judges declare guilty must pay back double to his neighbor'. But the sanction described in Ex. 22:4 is only applicable if the stolen animal is still alive. In case of selling or slaughtering the animal, he must pay back five head of cattle for the ox end four sheep for the sheep (Ex. 22:1). Is this case not more applicable for Job's situation? Prov. 6:31 even says that the robber must pay sevenfold! Anyhow, at least it becomes clear that the double compensation proves Job did not earn the loss of all his wealth.

he perished in his righteousness. Therefore Job was questioning Gods justice. But God makes Job feel that He also transcends Job's thought pattern and ideas of justice. God's justice prevails even if He acts in another way then we suppose Him to do[14]. Eventually, Job is forced to recognize God as his superior and admit that he went beyond his limits (Job 42:3).

Aware of each individual horizon of understanding (see below), it was proposed to the counselee that we read the book of Job together. As opposed to taking the (hermeneutic) lead, I as pastor adopted an attitude of cautious guidance. Together we purposed to be led by the book of Job and in a sphere of all openness discover, where possible, connections with Job's experience of suffering and her own concrete life story, inviting her also to (learn to) candidly express to God all her faith and life questions in a quest for the living God.

Connecting horizons (hermeneutic concept)

Horizon of understanding is a concept from the field of hermeneutics, first introduced by Hans Georg Gadamer. Instead of referring to 'frames of thought', he chose the broader term: 'horizons of understanding'. Everyone brings along his own background in the process of understanding. Whenever we open ourselves up and experience or learn something new, our horizon expands.[15] The wider our horizon, the greater the chance of increased understanding. The process of an encounter between two people is considered successful when horizons fuse. Just to be perfectly clear, Gadamer is not referring to a joining in which one horizon absorbs the other. The horizons do not merge and can never become one (Gadamer 1965,

---

14 > 14. Gert Kwakkel, 2013, Job tussen God en het kwaad, in: *Als geen Ander. De God van de profeten, een bundel opstellen.* Barneveld, passim.
15 cf. Charles Taylor 1989, *The Sources of the Self,* where he speaks of 'horizons of significance'

289–290, 356–357). Each person, so to speak, retains his/her own identity and horizon of experience. The different horizons touch each other and subsequently start expanding. In order to prevent the misunderstanding of 'merging', I would like to coin a new phrase: connection of horizons. 'Merging' essentially comes down to unification, in which a new entity is formed that is undistinguishable or difficult to unravel. It is doubtful whether the counselee and the counselor are able to connect that closely. 'Connection' indicates communality as well as diversity. I interpret *connecting of horizons* as an encounter in which the different identities shape one another while remaining intact, in a dynamic relationship.[16]

Connecting two horizons is seeking common ground between the horizons of two persons in order to come to an understanding (Thisselton 1980). This hermeneutic attitude demands an unbiased and open-minded attitude towards the other person's views. For this reason, it was agreed that Naomi would lead in the reading of Job, so that the pastor and theologian was compelled to put aside his own initial interpretations of Job as well as theodices.[17] It is important to realize that the pastor's own hermeneutic understanding of the Book of Job also plays a role. Furthermore, it is just as much an encounter between the counselee and the pastor's horizon of understanding formed from his own Christian background and experience of suffering.

The pastor was present, not in a leading, but in a following and accompanying role to help clarify and verbalize what

16 It can be looked at as a convergent perspective: multiple perspectives from different angles meet at a point, like two people both experiencing the sunset, one from Vancouver Island and the other from the Los Angeles beach.

17 In this we take Ganzevoort's warning seriously, in which he states (Ganzevoort 2005) that the problem with theodicy concepts is that they want to rescue God from the charges, leaving the victim to pay the price. An apologetic stance leads to a repeated undermining of the self-confidence and, in the worst case, will lead to a renewed trauma.

seemed to be happening to Naomi, bringing also alternative interpretations at her request. In doing so the pastor's own hermeneutic understanding: his initial exegesis, underwent a shift under the influence of the process that the counselee went through as well as the mutual journey undertaken by the pastoral counselor and counselee. A dialogical hermeneutic process took place within the counselee, between the counselee and the pastor and within the pastor himself. In other words: the pastor also changed through this counseling and his own horizon also grew wider and deeper. In fact, in this dialogical dynamic process a discerning hermeneutic took place: in a critical attitude towards the pastor, towards the former hermeneutics and towards the context of pastor and counselee.[18]

> Further literature study revealed that Charles V. Gerkin advocated a similar hermeneutic approach to pastoral care. He sees pastoral care as the encounter between the counselee's horizon of understanding and the counselor's. This horizon of understanding consists of the central life story that each person constructs by continually giving meaning to events happening to you and experiences gained. The pastor listens to the counselee's life questions and tries to make a connection with the Christian narrative. In the encounter between counselor and counselee a joining of horizons can take place. For Gerkin (Gerkin 1997) it is essential that the horizons of understanding are open to change and to re-interpretation. God's active involvement in the lives and horizons of understanding of both counselee and counselor plays an essential role in the possibility of re-interpretation (Vandenhoek 2007).

The hermeneutic approach that I advocate presupposes a fundamental openness to the message of the Holy Scriptures as well as the reality one faces. One should be open to the guidance of God's Spirit, who makes the connection between all the different

18 These observations were derived from certain marginal notes on this paper made by Dr. H. Geertsema (JDzn).

horizons of understanding. It is not theology that determines the kerygma (= the gospel message), but the testimony of faith in God (i.e. experienced in life). Formulated as: an expedition to allow the violated spirituality to be shaped by God's Spirit through the reading of the Book of Job, ultimately bringing it into connection with Christ, the suffering Righteous, who has borne every trauma and is able to sympathize with any weakness.

Chapter 2: A description of the pastoral route

1. The encounter: two horizons approach each other

The initiative to read and process the Book of Job together was taken jointly. In addition, Naomi could set the tempo, choose the texts and share and discuss how she processed them. The benefit of this approach was that the use of Naomi's own insights stimulated her own thought processes and decreased her feelings of powerlessness.

The encounter of both horizons, i.e. Naomi's concrete life history and Job's history, appeared to be a very tense process. The first reading soon stranded on constant 'triggers' arising from the first three chapters of Job, which reactivated her traumas: the unexpected attack of evil, God's active permission of evil, the loss of loved ones, impairment of health, the opposition of 'Mrs. Job', etcetera. This experience gave rise to the sketch *Access denied* [fig.1a].

Figure1a. Despondently she looks ahead and dreads the route, which is full of barbed wire and 'triggers'. "Access denied", English, though not the native language was chosen as a form of dissociation. The question is: who is refusing access? She does not permit herself to undertake the journey.

After six months a second attempt was undertaken [fig. 1b]. This time, we agreed to do a very reserved reading (scanning through the text without absorbing the details) of the first chapters. This led to a first step on the way to making a connection with Job's experiences of suffering.

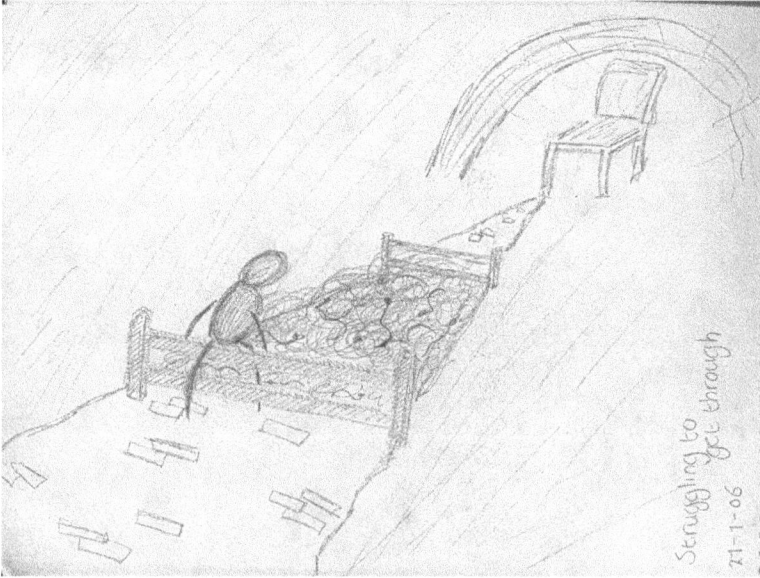

Figure 1b. Here a new effort is made to undertake the journey filled with triggers: struggling to get through...

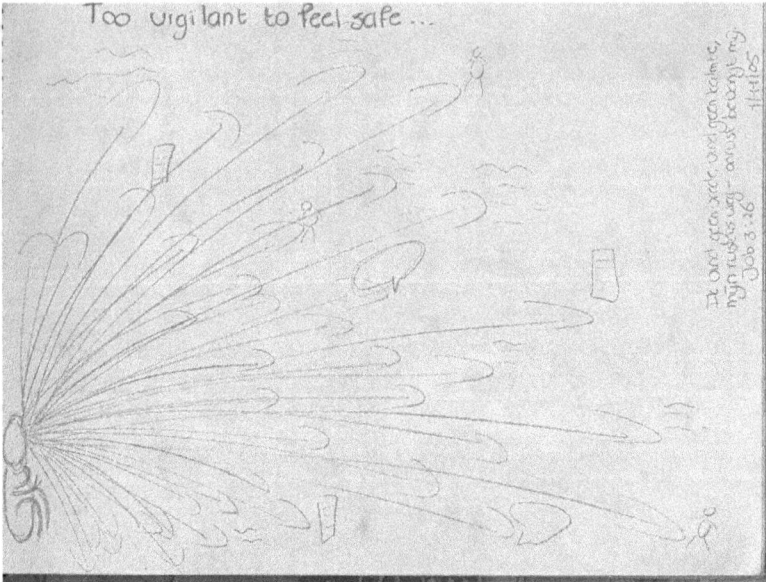

'I have no peace, no quietness; I have no rest, but only turmoil.'
(Job 3:26) Too vigilant to feel safe [fig. 2]

Figure 2 'Too vigilant to feel safe...': constantly in hypervigilance and arousal. Counselee has been forced into a corner... recognizes herself in Job's exclamations in Job 3 as she finds no peace, only restlessness. She holds everything at bay: people, the Word, statements made by others...

'What strength do I have, that I should still hope? What prospects, that I should be patient? Do I have the strength of stone? Is my flesh bronze?' (Job 6:11–12) [fig. 3]

Figure 3. The metaphor of suffering as the weight of a heavy stone appeals to her. Do I have any power to help myself? To a grieving person, the sense of grief is not clear, because it does not bring back the lost person. She is caving in under the burden, everything is headed downhill and everything her faith comprises — Bible, fellow-Christians, Cross, Church — all crumbles before her.

During her search Naomi gradually dared to recognize herself more and more as standing in the midst of an unbearable reality. She became able to momentarily suppress the reflex to deny and flee from this reality. In an earlier stage in her life she had fled into a religious experiment in which she allowed the trauma no room to exist. Through auto-mutilation she tried with all her might to keep the trauma out of the religious domain. Now she begins, very carefully, to draw a few lines in Job's direction.

The pastoral role was to encourage Naomi along the road towards her traumas, with the purpose of bringing her to acknowledge their reality and have the courage to make some sort of connection with Job. In other words, the different horizons were carefully unfolded to enable approach so that a true encounter could take place. In connecting with Job's horizon, Naomi would come to understand her own suffering. Although Job's person and experience is unique, the reality of his suffering is described in language which anyone in a context of suffering can identify with. His language guided Naomi as she learned to express the damage done to her wholeness.

Naomi's struggle was twofold. For her there were two more or less separate worlds; she could not reconcile her pain with her existence before God. The first identification with Job's defiant outcries of anguish evoked a fear of God's rejection within Naomi. At the same time, however, Job's provocative and aggrieved language began the gradual process of dismantling the wall dividing these two worlds [fig.4a and b]. And the process of the first stage in trauma recovery (stabilizing, recognizing and acknowledging) ended with replacing this wall with a more fluid boundary.

Fig. 4a. In all sorts of ways she feels enclosed or boxed-in, and she wonders who she really is. Part of her wishes to draw hope from God's Word but a wall prevents the words from reaching her. The cross (which ought to grant opening) is blocked because she cannot bear the thought of suffering. Fellow humans who could be a support to her are experienced as obstacles.

Fig. 4b. shows the dissociation from another perspective, where the 'triggers' are attacking her and she is 'cornered', barricading herself for protection. The cloud above her is the — as she feels it — threatening presence of God.

Little by little Naomi dismantled the wall between her two worlds by making a connection with her pain and unspeakable suffering. It was hard work, but Naomi no longer felt compelled to flee from suffering. The border of her own suffering opened through the encounter with Job. In this way she connected with all that from which she had distanced herself initially. This connection proved to be the first step towards recovery.

2. Experiencing God as Adversary in his unfathomable mysteries

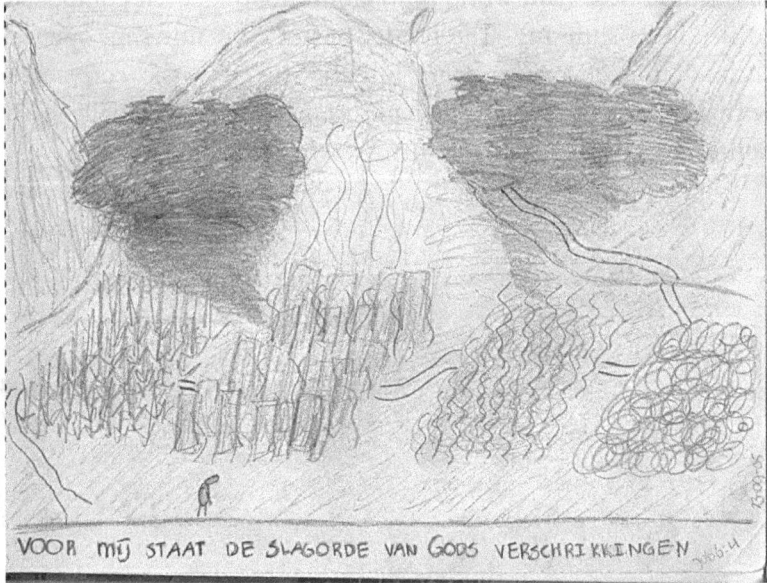

VOOR MIJ STAAT DE SLAGORDE VAN GODS VERSCHRIKKINGEN

'God's terrors are marshaled against me' (Job 6: 4) [fig. 5]

Fig. 5. Job speaks the words 'Gods terrors are marshaled against me'. She feels powerless and bends under the pressure. She dreads going into the mountains, full of 'trigger' areas. Also, the sky is threatening, there is a storm coming…! She shrinks from the confrontation with God.

'… I still dread all my sufferings, for I know you will not hold me innocent. Since I am already found guilty, why should I struggle in vain? '(Job 9:28–29) [fig. 6]

Fig.6. Naomi feels crushed by a presupposed rejection by God. I will never be found 'not guilty'. I will be condemned. Here shame and guilt are intertwining, as often is the case with victims of boundary violations.

'... The Almighty has terrified me' (Job 23:16b) [fig. 7]

Fig. 7. The Almighty has terrified me (Job 23:6b). Here two different worlds come into view. There is still an impenetrable veil between Naomi and her fellow Christians.

The next step towards understanding Job as an attacked and injured believer is that he sees God as his Adversary. Job openly dares to stand up to God. Naomi began to acknowledge that anger and disappointment with God formed a large part of her emotions. As a result, a severe conflict arose between her feelings and her conscience (her conscience was extremely powerful though deformed. It was only with great difficulty that she came to admit such feelings about God).

> *Job. Having read it, it feels as if some sort of contact was made. But with whom? Hm, I think with God, but it was via a detour. I can identify with Job. But in what?* (Naomi)

'He performs wonders that cannot be fathomed, miracles that cannot be counted.

When he passes me, I cannot see him; when he goes by, I cannot perceive him.

If he snatches away, who can stop him? Who can say to him, 'What are you doing?' (Job 9:10–12)

'Even if I summoned him and he responded, I do not believe he would give me a hearing. He would crush me with a storm and multiply my wounds for no reason'.

(Job 9:16–17)

> *Okay. That's what it feels like. Did God do this, did He wound me? My heart says yes, but my mind does not allow that answer. Who is speaking now? I know (I suddenly realize it): the 'wise' me. Again: did God wound me? Yes…*

> *Okay. That's what Job feels, and I identify with Job. The next logical step is: what emotions do I have? (…) This is scary, but the step must be taken. It's not until you say it, that the emotion can be set free. I can do it, I say: I am disappointed in God, and angry, I think. That last bit isn't proper, but I can't help it. Don't take it too harshly.* (Naomi)

From the perspective of pastoral counseling, this is a special moment in the trauma coping process (did He *injure* me?) Naomi's search to acknowledge the evil that overcame her may involve God himself. Every traumatized person is faced with the question why God let it happen and did not protect him or her. The book of Job grants the necessary space to ask these probing life questions dealing with the mysteries of God. Faith in God's omnipotence and goodness raises many questions in this context, but also provides space for them. Passionate complaints don't immediately put God's omnipotence in question but rather underline it. God is being addressed with respect to his deity! *The pastoral task, then, is not to stand in the way of the traumatized client with apologetics, as Job's friends do.* God does not need advocates to plead his case. And 'if God is God, we cannot judge him'. But because his nature is loving, good and trustworthy, He cannot possibly let evil pass unnoticed. He 'must' oppose it.

3. Ally and Adversary simultaneously!?

'For he wounds, but he also binds up; he injures, but his hands also heal.' (Job 5:18)

'Though he slay me, yet will I hope in him; I will surely defend my ways to his face.' (Job 13:15)

'My friends scorn me; my eye pours out tears to God, that he would maintain the right of a mortal with God as one does for a neighbor.' [NRSV] (Job 16:20–21) *(melitsay re'ay el eloah…. we yokach legeber 'im 'eloach)*

Already during the first reading this passage in Job 16:19–21 touched Naomi deeply. Job's declaration powerfully brought Naomi's horizon into contact with his and turned out to be crucial, leading to a new layer of understanding. Job's experience of suffering causes him to do (ask) the impossible: he appeals to God against God! God is called upon as judge and witness, because He was present at every event and allowed them to take place. *Job calls urgently upon God to defend him against God:* An enormous existential contradiction! God himself must defend his case against God. (This opens up a Christological perspective in the suffering).

These tension-packed declarations laid bare the connections in the midst of a confusing reality. The God of the past was *for* Naomi in the present. That was causing the tension [fig. 8]. How could He, the great Witness of her past, who saw all those frightening events, be for her now? He had actively permitted it to happen, certainly, not as the direct cause, but nevertheless.... Paradoxically enough, she experienced Him as Ally and Adversary simultaneously!

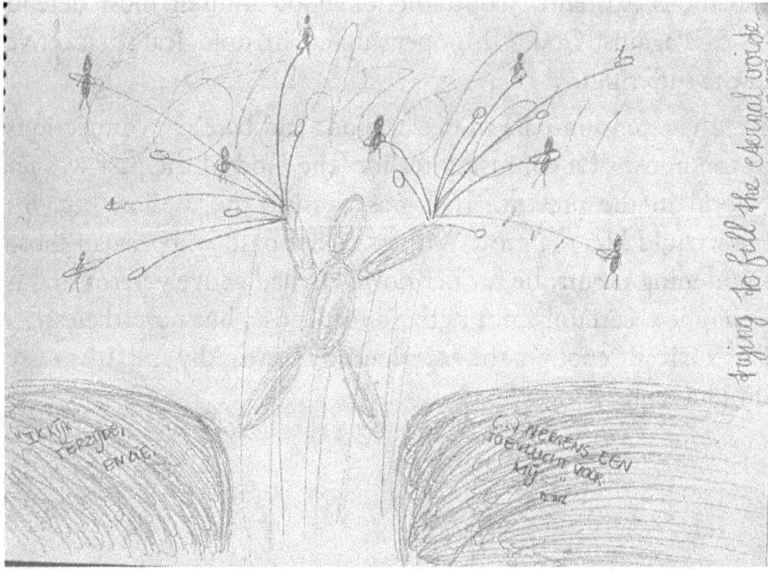

Fig. 8. 'Trying to fill the eternal void'. She tries to bridge the immense gap between past and present by several attempts to control. On the one side: 'Look to my right and see', on the other side: 'I have no refuge' (Ps. 142:4)

During the first reading, this realization caused a deep shock, which brought Naomi to the edge of a break-down ('The fuses blew!' she wrote somewhere). The cause of this short circuit was that multiple traumatic events were touched upon simultaneously. But at the same time, this conflict also brought contact, renewed identification, recognition, acceptance and acknowledgement. It was a violent confrontation that severely tested her nerves. This difficult process, however, was crucial to her acknowledging and connecting with her experiences of suffering.

> *It's as if there are two Gods, a God of then and a God of now. As Job says: "My eyes pour out tears to God; that he would maintain the right of a mortal with God"[NRSV] (Job 16: 20–21). On the one hand being drawn to God, wanting to go to Him; on the other hand repelled, wanting to be as far away from Him as possible, opposing Him. For He had been there, and let it happen... God as Witness. Literally. Being there, allowing it. This is very difficult.* (Naomi)

The way in which Naomi expressed herself remained quite rational. Nevertheless, it was an advance, however small. More and more, she was able to express her troubles to God.

Naomi realized full well that she was dependent upon God, also in the whole process of psychotherapy, in the pastoral counseling and in her confrontations. On the one hand, she acknowledged that she was nowhere without God; on the other hand she struggled with God as Adversary, in her rejection, in her own guilt complex and feelings of shame. It is contradictory, without reason. The great art of life is to allow the tension to exist, to bear it and to accept it.

During the following cautious approach toward the trauma through reading the book Job, this existential contradiction cropped up again. Two texts played a role, independently from each other: Job 3:8a and 9:12b on the one hand, and Psalm 143:8a on the other [fig. 9].

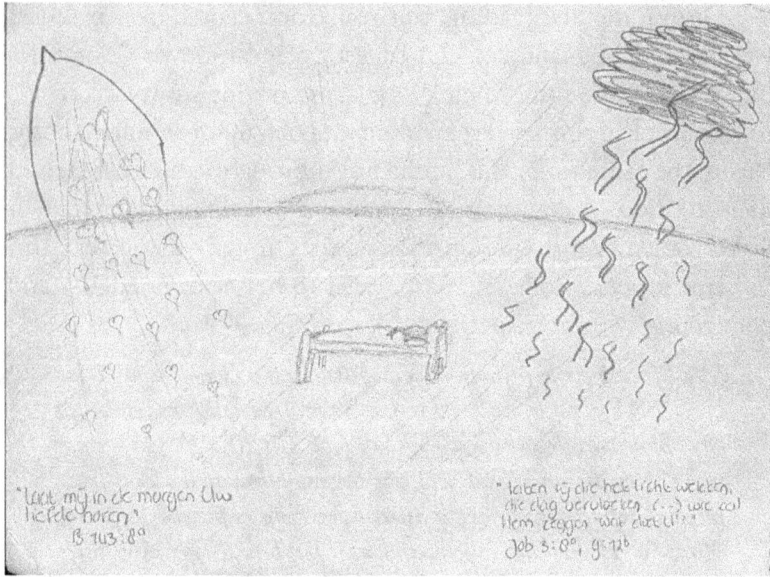

'May those who curse days curse that day, those who are ready to rouse Leviathan'(Job 3:8).

'Who can say to him, "What are you doing?"' (Job 9:12b)

'Let the morning bring me word of your unfailing love, for I have put my trust in you'(Ps.143:8a)

Fig. 9. Here the two worlds meet. The longing to hear God's voice in the morning, his love is never tardy (Psalm 143:8); longing for God's nearness. But at the same time: may those who curse days, curse that day. (from Job 3; were that I had never been born!) Who can and will challenge God to account for himself, saying: what are you doing? (Job 9:12).

This contradiction also came to the fore in yet another attempted approach as we see in the next drawing. It shows two thrones and two Bible texts with Naomi standing in between [fig. 10]. That clearly illustrates the duality. On the one hand, God as Witness, who allowed the events to take place; on the other hand, God as Ally and Helper. Both were present: sometimes more as Witness, at other times more as Ally. *Sometimes there was nothing, no feeling at all: emptiness, or perhaps tranquility in the midst of turmoil (Naomi).*

Job 9:17a placed alongside Psalm 142:7 (Naomi).

'He would crush me with a storm'(Job 9:17a)

'Set me free from my prison, that I may praise your name. Then the righteous will gather about me because of your goodness to me (Psalm 142:7).

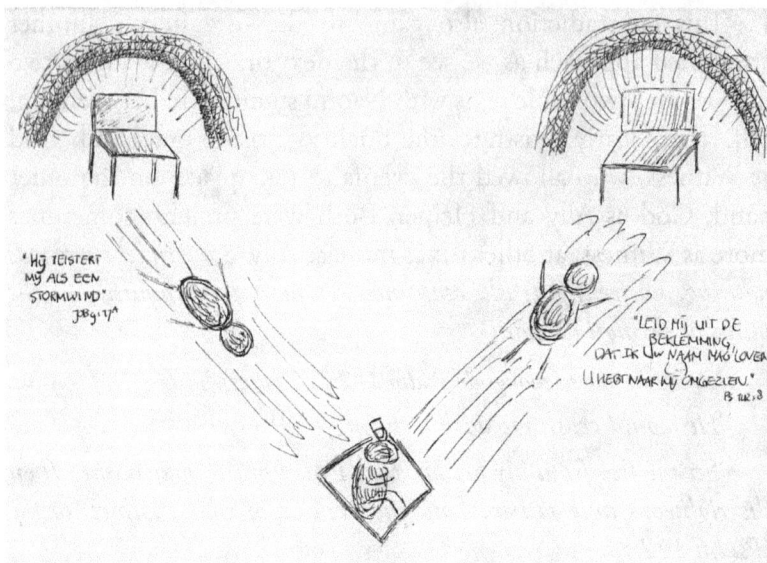

Fig. 10. Once again we see two representations of God's judgment throne, and the anxiety of having to account for oneself (a complex of guilt feelings and shame); with clashing longings. On the one hand God rages like a storm, who would feel safe? She has the irresistible urge to shut herself into a closed small space. At the same time the longing to appeal to Gods' power to liberate her from that stifling space. And we are able to recognize that the living God has looked out for her.

4. Recognition and liberation

Along the way there came moments of recognition which were liberating. These moments were neither planned nor programmed. The history of the following text has a long tradition and plays a well-known musical role: *'I know that my redeemer lives...'* (Job 19:25). In the joining of Job's and Naomi's horizons, faint shimmers of light appeared, though the pendulum kept swinging to and fro from this text, advancing and pulling away from it.

> *I bring up Job 19, because it has a sentence that struck me. Right in the middle of a passage full of complaints, and after Job says to his friends: "Why do you pursue me as God does?" he says: "but I know that my redeemer lives." That came as a complete surprise to me. Not easy to read, either. (Naomi).*

> *Elihu: he wants to show Job a different route. Defends God too, as the friends do. But differently; he wants to show Job the route of a mediator, 33:23.* "Then, if there should be for one of them an angel, a mediator, one of a thousand, one who declares a person upright (Naomi) [NRSV] (mediator, *melits... cf. Job 16:19–21).*

These little shimmers of light pulled her towards freedom. What a promising message! Still Naomi kept saying to herself: 'too good to be true'. The pastor carefully asked: "Could it also be 'too good *not* to be true!'?"

The final chapters of the Book of Job are an invitation to freedom and to identification with the sufferer. Job realizes he has crossed a certain line and the Creator himself corrects him. Even this exemplary trustworthy servant of God is not able to maintain a fitting balance in his experience of God as Adversary. After God's impressive revelation in which he confronts Job with a whole series of 'impossible' questions (chapters 38–39), Job can do no more than put his hand over his mouth (Job 40:4–5). "God's speeches may be read as indirect speech acts questioning the felicity conditions of Job's question" (Geeraerts 2003, 46)[19]. Job does not receive explanations of the mysteries of his suffering. He has not the right to question the righteousness of Gods counsel. The justice of God surpasses all our patterns and logic of what is righteous.

> All right, let's look at Elihu first: in my opinion (Naomi) the gist of his story is that God never acts unjustly. Is he saying that what Job said is wrong? And in the last part, isn't God also saying that Job was in the wrong? But if I have to read that, it's as if the door that was just beginning to open up a little (of starting to be able to …kind of… express anger towards God) has to be shut again. (Naomi).

It is amazing that it is God *Himself* who defends Job against his friends, who have been presenting themselves as God's advocates. God shows that He is Job's Ally in this suit, because Job has spoken straightforwardly and honestly about Him; that is, also in his rebelliousness. Naomi could not stop asking herself whether she was as honorable as Job. This distinguished the horizons from each other, but could also cause short-circuiting or alienation.

> Job says somewhere that he hasn't sinned and therefore stands in the right before God. That gives me the feeling that… (here the irritating 'me' crops up) Job has a right to voice his complaint to God, and I (Naomi) do not. But according to the pastor Job is saying that he is innocent, though it is his friends who force him to say that by their statement that God never punishes without cause, that Job must have done something that called for punishment. By the way, Job does admit that he is not without blemish: he was born in sin, from his mother's womb (Job 14:4). God also acknowledges that no blame can be found in Job to cause his suffering (Job 2:3). (Naomi)

> And God (…) will say in the end that Job was the only one to do

---

19 "Felicity conditions are criteria that have to be fulfilled if a speech act is to be properly made."

Him justice; he did not break the covenant. Certainly, Job cursed his
day of birth, but he did not curse God. Through it all, he searched
for Him. So I (Naomi) think that I have difficulty reading this be-
cause I then think I also have to understand it all. And that it has
to fit into my system, that this then is 'the answer'. Well it's not...
in the end you just start all over again, a new layer presents itself.
There are but two conclusions at the end: 1) that even being allowed
to be angry with God is grace; 2) that there is only one road: the
road of the cross (atonement). (Naomi).

The horizon of Job's suffering and that of the counselee
sometimes began in this way to diverge. In this you see that the
individuality of the situation and the context are not interwoven,
but remain distinct and retain their uniqueness. This largely
follows from the complexity of the concrete situation in which
the intertwining of bereavement, grief, dissociation, guilt and
shame plays an important role.

Can I truly identify with Job? Job knew why he was angry with
God. Do I (Naomi) know why I am angry? (...) I feel all sorts
of pits opening and alarm bells ringing (...) Would I be able to
write it down? Hm... I don't know ... We try a different approach.
The pastor says: for Job it was about loss, that he thought it wasn't
fair that he had to lose everything (children, possessions, health).
Is it about loss for you too? (...) painful (...) but I can handle it.
I say: yes! But now everything within me begins to revolt. I feel
all sorts of anxieties stirring deep within me, and all the alarm
signals start flashing. (Naomi)

5. Panorama

There is still a long way to go, but the recovery process has
started and has moved towards acceptance, connection and
communality (phases from Herman). Naomi has ventured on
that road, acknowledging the guidance of the Spirit of Christ,
who as the great Hermeneut (Interpreter) invites us to ask

the urgent questions of life, and brings about the connection between different horizons of understanding. Together with Job we came to acknowledge that we are dealing with 'things I did not understand, things too wonderful for me to know. (…) My ears had heard of you but now my eyes have seen you'. (Job 42:3 and 5).

This perspective fits into the panorama of the work of Jesus, the Righteous One par excellence who suffered and overcame. Initially Naomi did not dare to pray together in the pastoral setting, which meant praying for her in her absence instead of with her. But little by little prayer started playing a part in the pastoral process. Further along the route, there came more space to bring the questions about suffering into connection with Jesus Christ, also through prayer, and especially to effectively name the evil (abuse) under which He suffered so deeply. She was then able to respond to Jesus' invitation to identify with Him, the greater than the suffering Job. (Hebr. 5:7–10). The mystery of God (God above me) taking it up against God (God with me) has ultimately become reality in the unique suffering of Jesus Christ. He is the Judge-Witness in the suit 'God versus God' (using Job's words), as between a man and his friend (Job 16:19–21). He is, more than Job, the Righteous One, and at the same time, the Mediator, who suffered the most, but triumphed. Oh, the depth of the riches of the profound wisdom and unsearchable knowledge of God! The ultimate revelation of how seriously Jesus takes traumas is that after His resurrection, with a *glorified* body he shows the wounds of his suffering (Luke 24:40).

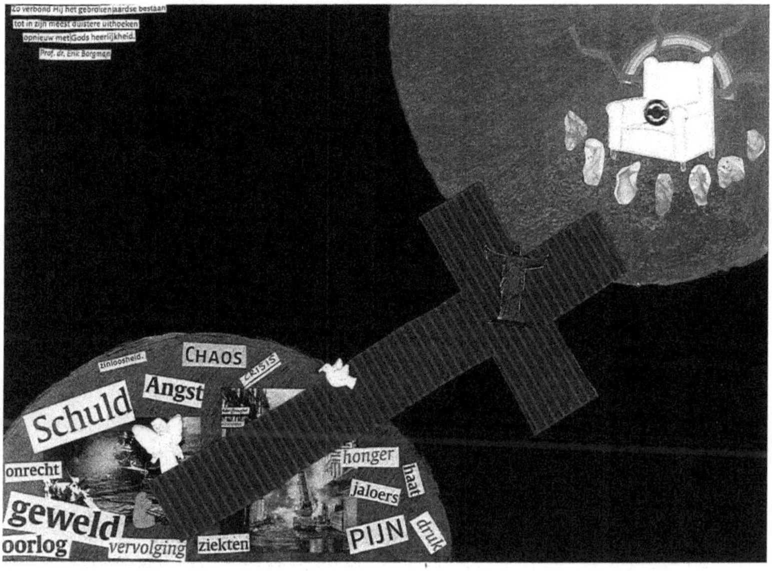

Marco van Eyck 2012

Fig. 11. 'In this way He reconnected the broken earthly existence with God's glory until the darkest corners' (dr. Erik Borgman). The redemptive work of Christ in his suffering, who was able to connect the glory of God with a world full of traumas. 'War, Violence, Injustice, Guilt, Fear, Chaos, Meaningless, Crisis, Persecution, Diseases, Pain, Jealousy, Famine'.

Conclusion

I n the context of trauma, the pastoral counselor is called to operate next to other caregivers from his own field of competence. This can be of benefit to the trauma-coping process and supplement the caregiving. Consultation with the other specialists is of eminent importance for working synchronously. Should that not be the case then both the therapy and the pastoral counseling will be much less effective. For a healthy point of departure three elements are required: a safe setting, a guaranteeing the counselee's autonomy and a 'non-anxious presence' in which one does not ignore unspeakable suffering.

Pastoral counseling in the context of posttraumatic stress disorder demands great patience, caution and restraint. The pastor can be specifically helpful by adopting an open attitude towards the most penetrating questions about suffering, without taking an apologetic stance. The language of Job proved to be very useful for expressing the experience of suffering and asking penetrating life questions. The book of Job helps to understand and express feelings evoked in a traumatic context, especially in the relationship with God. The faith experience in Job's suffering is crucial in all its mysteries: God as Adversary and God as Ally. Naomi encountered the God of Job in a comparable experience. This encounter helped her in the healing process of her trauma wounds and in the caring of her scars. It cannot be guaranteed that this will always be the case, nor can it be claimed that the Book of Job is suitable for all trauma coping. In addition, not every horizon connection will be the same and lead to a connection or joining.

We have seen here two horizons come together: that of Job and that of the counselee. These two horizons come together, intertwine, and at times diverge again. In the end each retains its independence, does not merge, but comes to a meeting of minds. Though the experiences of suffering may be comparable, distinction remains. We see two directions opening: one leading to the horizon as presented in the Book of Job, the other leading to the life-story of the counselee. Between these two horizons, in Naomi's understanding of Job's suffering, a connection takes place with her own horizon, her own suffering.

The pastor's action should be characterized by willingness to serve, openness and caution. He should not force anything, but should let the other be herself as much as possible. Carefully, and in the counselee's tempo, he looks for points of contact between the traumas and experiences of suffering. The most important part of the trauma coping process is helping the counselee to connect with memories, pain and anxiety. These are brought into relationship with (the) God (of Job), the other and one's self. Along the route, the counselee is implicitly and explicitly invited to restore the connection, so that she no longer needs to flee suffering, but is able to connect with everything from which she had initially distanced herself. Making these connections is the route to healing. It perforates the isolation and lessens the loneliness. In the treatment and care of the wounds, the pastor is called upon to show love, compassion and patience, following Christ.

Reference List

Aarts, P.G.H. and W.D. Visser. 2007. *Trauma: diagnostiek en behandeling*. Houten: Boon.

Bommerez, Jan. and van Zijtveld, Kees. 2008. *Kun je een rups leren vliegen?* :23–25. Eemnes: Nieuwe dimensies.

Brink, Egbert. 2004. Compassie in gebrokenheid (= compassion in brokenness). In *Meer dan genoeg. Het verlangen naar meer van de Geest*, eds. H. ten Brinke and J.W. Maris. Barneveld : De Vuurbaak: 54–67.

—, 2009. Pour une approche pastorale dans le contexte post-traumatique. *La Revue réformée* 60 no. 251: 67–80.

Friedman, Edwin H. 2007. *A Failure of Nerve: Leadership in the Age of the Quick Fix*. New York: Seabury Books.

Gadamer, Hans Georg. 1965. *Wahrheit und Methode*. Tübingen: J.C.B. Mohr.

Ganzevoort, Ruard R. 2005. Als de grondslagen vernield zijn… Over trauma, religie en pastoraat. *Praktische theologie* 32, no. 2: 344–361. http://www.ruardganzevoort.nl (accessed July 3, 2012).

—, 2009. All things work together for good. Theodicy and post-traumatic spirituality. In *Secularization Theories, Religious Identity, and Practical Theology*, ed. W. Gräb and L.

Charbonnier, 183–192. Münster: LIT-Verlag.

—, 2011. Trauma en spirituele verzorging. *Cogiscope* no. 3 (November): 2–5.

Gerkin, Charles.V. 1997. *An Introduction to Pastoral Care.* Nashville: Abingdon Press.

Herman, Judith. 1992. Complex PTSD: A syndrome in survivors of prolonged and repeated trauma. *Journal of Traumatic Stress* 5 no. 3: 377–391.

—, 2001 (1997 revised ed.). T*he Aftermath Of Violence — From Domestic Abuse To Political Terror in Trauma and Recovery.* New York: Basic Books.

Jones, J.W. 1991. *Contemporary Psychoanalysis and Religion: Transference and Transcendence.* New Haven. CT: Yale University Press.

Langberg, D.M. 1999. *On the Treshold of Hope: Opening the Door to Healing for Survivors of Sexual Abuse.* Illinois: Tyndale House Publishers

—, 2002. Coping with Traumatic Memory. *Marriage and Family: A Christian Journal,* 5 (4), 447–456.

—, 2003. *Counseling Survivors of Sexual Abuse.* Xulon Press.

LeDoux, J. 1996. *The Emotional Brain. The Mysterious Underpinnings of Emotional Life.* New York: Simon & Schuster.

—, 2002. *The Synaptic Self. How our Brains Become Who We Are.* Harmondsworth: Viking.

Lifton, Robert Jay. 1979. *The Broken Connection: On Death and the Continuity of Life*. New York: Simon & Schuster.

Matsakis, Aphrodite. 1992. *I Can't Get Over It! A Handbook for Trauma Survivors*. Oakland: New Harbinger Publishers.

Mathewson, Dan. 2006. Death And Survival in the Book of Job: Desymbolization And Traumatic Experience. In *Library of Hebrew Bible/Old Testament Studies T & T Clark library of biblical studies* 450. New York: T & T Clark. http://books.google.nl/books/about/Death_And_Survival_in_the_Book_of_Job.html?id=R5gvC7JfQ9AC&redir_esc=y (accessed on 13 July 2012)

McNamara, P. 2009. *The Neuroscience of Religious Experience*. New York: Cambridge University Press.

Roukema-Koning, Barbara. 1998. Relationele zelf-ervaringen en spreken over God. Een psychologie van het "Zelf" als hermeneutisch instrument. In *De Praxis als verhaal*. Narrativiteit en Praktische theologie, 43–64. Kampen: Kok.

Scott, M.J. 2007. *Moving On After Trauma*. New York: Routledge.

Siegel, Daniel. 1999. *The Developing Mind. How Relationships and the Brain Interact to Shape Who We Are*. New York: Guilford Press.

Thisselton, Anthony C. 1980. *The Two Horizons*. Exeter: The Paternoster Press.

—, 2009. *Hermeneutics, An Introduction*. Grand Rapids: Eerdmans.

Taylor, Charles. 1989. The Sources of the Self, The Making of the Modern Identity. Cambridge: Harvard University Press.

Van den Blink Han. 1998. Trauma Reactivation in Pastoral Counseling: Implications for Theory and Practice. American Journal of Pastoral Counseling 1 no.2, 23–38.

—, 2004. Late Vocation: A Personal Reflection. The Anglican Catholic XVI (Summer): 22–44.

—, 2010. Traumaverwerking en spiritualiteit. Psyche & Geloof 21, no. 1: 20–32.

Vandenhoeck, Anne. 2007. *De meertaligheid van de pastor in de gezondheidszorg. Resultaatgericht pastoraat in dialoog met het narratief-hermeneutisch model van C.V. Gerkin.* diss., Katholieke Universiteit Leuven.

Wertheim-Cahen, Truus. 2007. De rol van vaktherapieën bij de behandeling van psychotrauma. In *Trauma: diagnostiek en behandeling,* 313–327.

Winnicott, Donald.1960. Theory of the parent-child relationship. *International Journal of Psycho-Analysis* 41: 585–595.

Wright, H. Norman. 2011. *The Complete Guide to Crisis & Trauma Counseling.* Ventura CA: Regal.

Studies on Job

Bijl, Cor. 1995. *Zo rijk als Job.* Kampen: Voorhoeve.

Blom, Cornelis. 2009. *Zonder grond onder de voeten,* Een theologische analyse van het boek Job en Genesis 1–4 vanuit het perspectief van het kwaad in de schepping. Zoetermeer: Boekencentrum.

Clines, D. J. A. 1989. *Job 1–20,* Word Biblical Commentary. Tenessee: Thomas Nelson.

—, 2006. *Job 21–37,* Word Biblical Commentary. Tenessee: Thomas Nelson.

—, 2006. *Job 38–42,* Word Biblical Commentary. Tenessee: Thomas Nelson.

De Jong, Henk, ed. 1977, 1994. Wijsheid en openbaring – Beschouwing over het boek Job. In: Begeleidend schrijven, 25 jaar Theologische Studiebegeleiding, ed. H. de Jong and J. Bouma. Amsterdam: Buijten & Schipperheijn, 37–48.

Geeraerts, Dirk. 2003. Caught in a web or irony: Job and his embarrassed God. In: Ellen van Wolde (red.), *Job 28. Cognition in Context.* 37–55. Leiden: Brill.

Gordis, Robert 1978. *The Book of Job: Commentary,* New Translation and Special Studies. Jerusalem: JTS Press.

Hartley, J.E. 1988. *The Book of Job,* New International

Commentary on the Old Testament. Grand Rapids: Eerdmans.

Horst, F. 1968, *Hiob* (ch. 1–18), Biblischer Kommentar Altes Testament. Neukirchen-Vluyn: Neukirchener Verlag.

Lévêque, J. 2001. *Le mal de Job, dans Le mystère du mal, péché, souffrance et rédemption*, Toulouse: éd. M.-B.Borde, Éditions du Carmel.

Longman III, Tremper. 2012. *Job*, Baker Commentary on the Old Testament Wisdom and Psalms Categories: Job. Grand Rapids: Baker Academic Published.

Magary, D.R. 2009. Job. In: Series: *NIV Application Commentary.* Grand Rapids: Zondervan.

Strauss, H. 1969. *Hiob - XVI/2 (ch. 19:1–42:17), Biblischer Kommentar Altes Testament.* Neukirchen-Vluyn: Neukirchener Verlag.

Van der Beek, A. 1992. *Rechtvaardiger dan God. Gedachten bij het boek Job.* Nijkerk: Callenbach.

Van der Dussen, A. 1998. *Job: Geloven en lijden om niet.* Amsterdam: Buijten & Schipperheijn.

Van Selms, A. 1984. *Job, een praktische bijbelverklaring.* Kampen: Kok.

—, 1982. *Job, Deel 1, Prediking van het Oude Testement.* Nijkerk: Callenbach.

—, 1983. *Job, Deel 2, Prediking van het Oude Testement.* Nijkerk: Callenbach.